Snowmobiles

Quinn M. Arnold

seedlings

CREATIVE EDUCATION • CREATIVE PAPERBACKS

Published by Creative Education and Creative Paperbacks
P.O. Box 227, Mankato, Minnesota 56002
Creative Education and Creative Paperbacks
are imprints of The Creative Company
www.thecreativecompany.us

Design by Ellen Huber; production by Mary Herrmann
Art direction by Rita Marshall
Printed in the United States of America

Photographs by iStockphoto (DIGIcal, Elviraga, FooTToo,
GibsonPictures, Imgorthand, kamski, KKIDD, Murmakova,
RomanBabakin, sara_winter, SergeyVButorin, treasurephoto, Ulga,
WesAbrams, wsmahar), Shutterstock (Delpixel, Garry2014, irina02,
Erkki Makkonen, Parilov, resilva)

Library of Congress Cataloging-in-Publication Data
Names: Arnold, Quinn M., author.
Title: Snowmobiles / Quinn M. Arnold.
Series: Seedlings.
Includes index.
Summary: A kindergarten-level introduction to the motorized
vehicles known as snowmobiles, covering their purpose,
parts, and operation, and such defining features as their
runners and tracks.
Identifiers: LCCN 2018053212 / ISBN 978-1-64026-173-0
(hardcover) / ISBN 978-1-62832-736-6 (pbk) /
ISBN 978-1-64000-291-3 (eBook)

Subjects: LCSH: Snowmobiling—Juvenile literature. /
Snowmobiles—Juvenile literature.
Classification: LCC GV856.5.A76 2019 / DDC 796.94—dc23

CCSS: RI.K.1, 2, 3, 4, 5, 6, 7; RI.1.1, 2, 3, 4, 5, 6, 7;
RF.K.1, 3; RF.1.1

First Edition HC 9 8 7 6 5 4 3 2 1
First Edition PBK 9 8 7 6 5 4 3 2 1

TABLE OF CONTENTS

Time to go!

Snowmobiles are used in cold places.

They drive on snow and ice.

Runners slide on top of the snow.

Handlebars steer the runners.

This turns the snowmobile.

A track is behind the runners.

It grips the ground. This moves the snowmobile forward.

The throttle makes the engine go.

The brake makes the snowmobile slow down.

throttle

Riders wear warm clothes and helmets.

A windshield blocks wind and snow.

The seat has room for one or two people.

A snowmobile goes
through woods and fields.
It zooms over snow and ice.

Headlights show
the path ahead.

Go, snowmobile, go!

Picture a Snowmobile

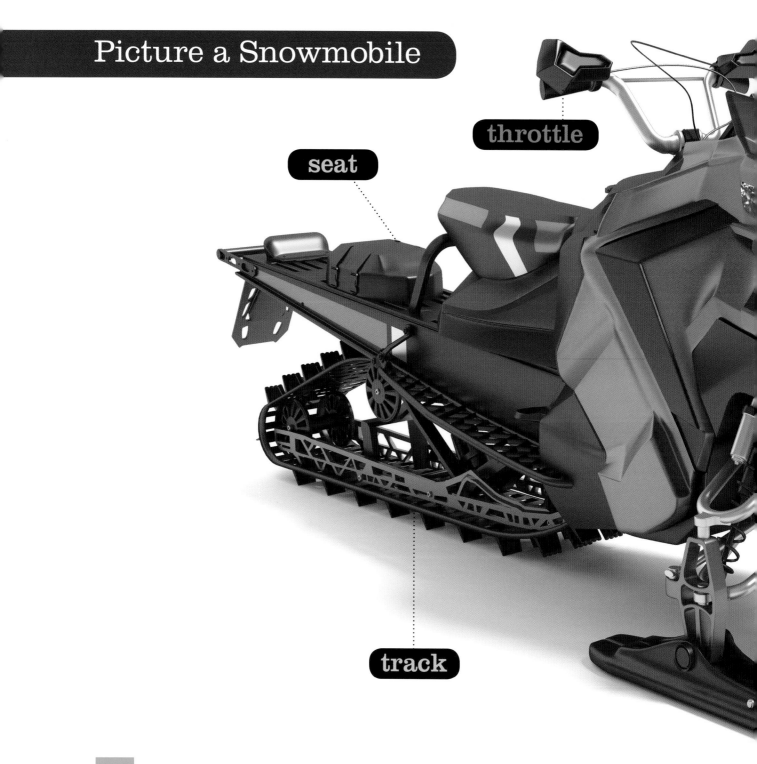

throttle

seat

track

brake

starter

handlebar

mirrors

runners

engine: a machine that provides power and makes something move

steer: to turn or guide the movement of a vehicle

throttle: the part that controls power to an engine

track: a big, strong belt that goes around a vehicle's wheels

Read More

Fortuna, Lois. *Snowmobiles*.
New York: Gareth Stevens, 2017.

Scheff, Matt. *Snowmobiles*.
Minneapolis: Abdo, 2015.

Websites

ISMA: Kid's Projects
http://www.snowmobile.org/snowmobile-projects-for
-kids.html
Print out pictures to color, make a paper model snowmobile,
and learn how to be a safe rider!

Printable Coloring Pages: Snowmobile
https://printablefreecoloring.com/drawings/transportation
/snowmobile-skidoo/
Print out pictures of snowmobiles to color.

Index